# TALKING WITH TECH:

## Solutions for Children and Adults

## Who Are Nonverbal

**By Betsy Furler, MS, CCC-SLP**

# CONTENTS

# FOREWORD

As I began writing this book, I wondered why some people are successful with augmentative and alternative communication (AAC) – and why are some not? Does it depend on the therapist, family support, or the device? What is the difference? I believe the difference is the approach – and the approach is different for everyone.

It's like a marathon. Training to run long distances is different for each person. If I trained for a marathon, I wouldn't expect to run those 26.2 miles overnight. I wouldn't judge my ability to complete a marathon based on my performance on Day One. And I wouldn't decide to give up on my marathon goal just because I failed to run the entire distance today. Instead, I would train and plan. I would spend weeks, months, and maybe years getting ready to run the distance. I would work on underlying behaviors, habits, and skills. I would incorporate stretching as well as developing skills like form, strength, and endurance. I would need to diet and definitely sleep more! I would run small distances at first and then longer distances with time. I would practice for many sessions, getting ready for marathon day.

AAC is like a marathon. It is not a quick fix. You shouldn't put a device in front of a child or adult who is nonverbal and expect them to converse with it immediately – but we do. We therapists assess children and adults, and if they fail to communicate with the device or app during the evaluation, we say they do not have the ability to use the device. We give up – on them and on ourselves. If I were assessed on my ability to run a marathon today, I would fail. I can run for about one minute, and that's it. However, my performance today doesn't mean a marathon is out of my reach. I have the potential to run those 26.2 miles, and – if I wanted – I could train and be successful.

Our kids can communicate. They communicate with their eyes and their bodies. We know they can communicate; we only need to help them find their words. AAC isn't simple. It isn't easy. It is a marathon, and we must start at a basic, early level and grow from there.

This book is written in honor and with thanksgiving for all the wonderful children and adults I have worked with during my 25 year career as a speech pathologist. You have taught me so much more than I taught you, and I am forever grateful!

# A NOTE TO PARENTS

Dedication is an important part of running a marathon and using AAC. Just like it's not always the right time to run a marathon, it may not always be the right time to start AAC. You must be dedicated. It's not easy, but it is worth it.

As a mom of a child with complex medical issues, I understand and respect how much families have on their plates. I remember when my son was an infant and the occupational therapist (OT) asked how often we were doing infant massage. I was already a speech pathologist. I worked in early intervention for years and was an expert in feeding and sensory integration. I knew the value of infant massage, especially for my preemie who had a neurological disorder – but *I could not* fit infant massage into our days. Even with my super-supportive husband and someone cleaning my house (although we had almost zero income at the time – that's another story – but someone cleaning my house has always been the #1 item on my budget, even above food!), I was still busy every minute of the day when my older son was an infant. I was feeding him 24/7, but he was a terrible nurser. I had professional expertise in feeding and the help of a lactation consultant, but the schedule was brutal. Every three hours, I nursed Henry and then bottle-fed him. I put him down for a nap and then pumped. As soon as I finished cleaning the pump and drank some water, he was awake and ready to start the cycle again. I might get a second to throw in a load of laundry since he "spit up" – or rather, projectile vomited – many times a day. We both went through many changes of clothing each day. When the OT mentioned infant massage, I just couldn't do it. There was no time or energy for infant massage, no matter how important it was. We were just barely surviving. Maybe your family is just surviving too. If so, know that I empathize and have been where you are.

You need to start AAC when you can commit to it. Without the commitment, you and your child will not be successful, and it will be frustrating and defeating. Commitment is very important, but the time has to be right.

When it is the right time, surround yourself with a lot of support. Connect with other families using AAC. I have a Facebook group for families that you can find out about on my website, communicationcircles.com. Read about AAC and make it a priority to learn as much as you can. It will become a habit and get easier as you progress; however, the first few months are usually challenging.

# INTRODUCTION

AAC is augmentative and alternative communication. It is also called "augcomm." AAC is the use of methods other than verbal speech to help people who are nonverbal communicate functionally. When I use the term "AAC," I most often mean use of technology – like iPads and tablets – to aid a user in communicating.

I believe everyone deserves a voice. My mission is to make AAC mainstream so everyone has access to augmentative communication. Did you know each of us is walking around with a communication device in our pockets? It's our smartphones, and all you need to do is download an app! I want everyone to know about this revolutionary technology. A child who is born with a disability, who is unable to speak verbally, or is unable to communicate functionally with their voice should have access to AAC. Adults with acquired disabilities – such as someone who's had a stroke or has ALS or Parkinson's disease – should also have access to these amazing tools. Another type of patient who frequently goes without the ability to communicate is someone temporarily unable to speak. These patients might have been intubated or are unable to talk for other medical reasons. If they have a smartphone, it is easy to access an augmentative communication app that turns any smartphone into an AAC device very inexpensively – possibly even for free! Let's spread the news about this technology that is now accessible to all. Everyone needs be aware of AAC if something happens to a loved one and they have a need for augmentative communication.

If you are already aware of augmentative communication and some of the available apps, you may have already starting using AAC. However, the two challenges families encounter most often are: (1) lack of appropriate support while implementing AAC, and (2) the device selected for the child or adult isn't a good fit. Other common issues are parents and/or the user not receiving proper training. Getting the user's community – such as a child's school district or an adult's workplace – on board can also be a challenge. When these challenges are present, AAC becomes a struggle.

Because of these common struggles, I want to make this book about getting *going* with AAC – even if you've already gotten started with AAC. I want this book to be relevant and informative and help you make progress toward your AAC goals. By reading this book, you will learn how to tweak your AAC experience so your child, patient, or loved one can communicate independently.

# WHO AM I?

Since we'll be spending quite a bit of time together as you read this book, I'd like to share a little about who I am and why AAC is important to me.

I grew up in Texas. I was born in Dallas. At the time, my parents lived in the nearby city of Terrell and they drove to Dallas for my birth. My father was an Episcopal minister, and we moved every few years because of his job. My mom has a masters degree in Christian education and also worked in churches, so I went to church a lot as a child!

I loved babies, even when I was a baby. I started babysitting at age ten and often cared for children with disabilities. In college, I even worked at a daycare for typical kids – it was awful! But I did an internship at an agency that provided therapeutic services for children with disabilities, and I loved it. In college, I double-majored in psychology and sociology with an undeclared minor in religion. I earned my bachelor's degree from Austin College and planned to go to graduate school. I originally wanted to be a psychologist, but after an internship at a drug rehab facility, I decided that profession was too stressful and I didn't want to spend my life listening to people's problems. I worked for a photographer for a year while I looked for grad schools. I wanted to live in Dallas with friends, so I enrolled in the University of Texas at Dallas. I had no idea what I wanted to study and had forgotten about that internship at the therapeutic agency. UT Dallas didn't have an elementary education program, but they told me about their great program in communication disorders – so I signed up. It was seriously unintentional, but it was perfect. I was an out-of-field student, but I ended up starting and finishing with my class and earned a teaching certificate (K-12 special education) in the process. During grad school, I discovered the kids I loved working with the most were the most complex kids.

I am speech pathologist by profession. I have 25 years of experience, both with speech pathology and with augmentative communication. I started using AAC when I was in grad school in the early 1990s. (I actually had a class that long ago in augmentative communication!) In grad school – and even now – I love getting people to talk and communicate.

I am a technology expert. I began using the iPod Touch in therapy as soon as it was released. I was not a tech savvy person back then, but as soon as I saw that now-iconic iPod commercial, I had to have one! I was amazed at how everything was controlled by tilting the device and swiping the touchscreen with just a finger. It sounds crazy now, but back then we did not have access to touchscreens commercially. The iPod Touch was revolutionary, and I bought one as soon as it was available.

I was working in an autism treatment facility at the time. In the evenings, I worked with adult patients who had suffered strokes or had Alzheimer's, Parkinson's disease, or other types of acquired disorders. I began using the iPod Touch in therapy with my adult patients. I downloaded some of the communication apps that were available, and suddenly I had a way to test a person's ability to use AAC without getting them one of the big, expensive, and clunky dedicated devices. It was so exciting!

Apple Corporation then released the iPad, and – of course – I had to have one of those too! I began using the iPad with both adult and pediatric patients for a variety of therapeutic goals. I learned the iPad is a great reward in itself, but what I really value most is its use for education and communication.

My experience with iPods and iPads has evolved into a love of apps. I love apps for several reasons. Apps are great for leveling the playing field for kids with minor and major disabilities. They help kids who are reluctant readers. They help kids and adults who cannot quite get organized. Apps really make a difference, and they change lives.

After I became obsessed with apps, I started delving into AAC apps and iPads. I began learning more about dedicated devices as I compared the new technology of iPads and tablets to the standard AAC solutions of the day. I became interested in eye gaze technology and started doing eye gaze evaluations on a regular basis about four years ago. At that time, the technology had improved immensely, and I was – and continue to be – fascinated with how eye gaze can unlock potential in people who are nonverbal and also unable to use their hands and arms effectively.

I continue to work with technology in communication, educational, and therapeutic realms. I love thinking about apps and how they can enhance everyone's lives. Because of this passion, I have coined myself "Your App Lady," and I blog about apps for improving everyday life at yourapplady.com.

I have autism training in Floortime/DIR, and I am an autism consultant that combines my knowledge of technology with my experience treating autism. I love using AAC with kids with autism – even the kids who are verbal but don't functionally use their language.

As for my family life, I have two sons: Henry and Sam. Henry is 19, and Sam is 13. Henry is medically fragile and had a life expectancy of one year – but he's made it all the way to college! Henry lives in a dorm with his service dog Scout and is doing great. Parenting Henry has taught me so much about being the parent of a special needs child, and I've become an expert in supporting the transition to adulthood and independence these past few years. Sam is my younger son. He's thirteen and in the seventh grade. Sam loves to play baseball. He plays the trumpet in the school band, as well as the cymbals in the drum line. Sam has a black belt in martial arts and is working on his second-degree black belt. I have Holly, a Yorkie, who is my little girl and often works with me. We all need an animal to keep us calm and focused. I am married to Eric. He works as a building contractor and does remodels and some handyman work.

With many nonverbal patients, AAC is miraculous. I can't wait to tell you more and help you become proficient using augmentative communication with your child, loved one, or patients.

# CHAPTER 1
# TYPES OF AAC

Alternative and augmentative communication (AAC) is anything used in addition to verbal speech for communication. Sign language and gestures are AAC. Body language and facial expressions are AAC. We all use AAC to express ourselves, but people who are nonverbal need AAC for all – or the majority of – their communication.

I categorize AAC into three types:

- **Low-tech AAC** – communicating with pictures, photos, written messages on paper, visual schedules, or objects / object exchange.

- **Mid-tech AAC** – communicating with electronic devices that utilize a low level of customization; these devices often feature physical buttons and a recorded voice.

- **High-tech AAC** – communicating with highly-customizable electronic devices with synthesized voices.

The distinction between high-tech and mid-tech AAC is an important one. While both are communication with electronic devices, high-tech AAC uses computers, iPads, and tablets that can be highly customized and are flexible to a user's needs as he or she progresses with their communication. Mid-tech AAC systems are not as robust. A mid-tech device would be something that looks like a box and usually has between nine to 32 buttons. Each button is programmed with one word or phrase, like "milk" or "juice." When the milk button is pushed, the device plays the recorded word "milk." As you can see just from this example, a mid-tech device is limiting. The user can only access a few pre-programmed buttons and cannot link them together into phrases or sentences. Even the recorded voices are limiting. Ideally, the recorded voice should match an approximation of the user's voice – that means if an eight year-old boy is using the device, the recorded voice should sound like an eight year-old boy. That is often not the case with mid-tech AAC devices.

High-tech AAC has gotten so inexpensive that I use it almost exclusively, and I believe everyone deserves to try high-tech AAC. Therefore, when I talk about augmentative communication or use the term AAC in my practice and in this book, I most often mean high-tech AAC – that is, communicating with computers, iPads, and tablets. I might use some low-tech AAC solutions in case a high-tech device breaks down or if you're in the water, at the beach, in the swimming pool, or in other situations where a high-tech device may be unusable or unavailable.

Current high-tech AAC devices include computers, iPads/tablets, and dedicated devices. These devices all require electricity and have dynamic screens, meaning they can switch among multiple screens. A large amount of vocabulary can be stored in these devices. High-tech AAC devices also have synthesized voices, meaning that as the user types text into the device, it will speak for the person. High-tech AAC has access to a wide range of voices – very important, as the voice should match the user and be a voice he or she identifies with and embraces.

High-tech AAC is further divided into the type of communication device used – dedicated devices or tablets. Let's learn more about both categories and examine the pros and cons of each:

## Dedicated Devices

A dedicated device is a computer (or even a tablet) that is only able to access an AAC application. It is unable to run any other program, software, app, and it cannot access the internet. A dedicated device is solely for communication. These devices are developed and manufactured with the special needs population in mind.

The main pro of a dedicated device is they are frequently funded by insurance. Because of insurance companies' financial assistance, some families prefer to purchase a dedicated device because they cannot afford or find funding for a tablet.

Another pro of a dedicated device is customer support through the manufacturer. Frequently, these companies have representatives all over the United States and other countries. Their representatives are available to go to the user's home, school, or place of employment to set up the device and help troubleshoot any technical problems. These manufacturers also have telephone support and frequently hold workshops and training for parents, users, and therapists.

Dedicated devices are also the easiest to mount on a wheelchair. The devices come with a wheelchair mount from the company that is easy to install and is quite secure. You can get mounts for tablets, but it can be a challenge to find one that is stable and a good fit.

A final pro is the best eye gaze technology is available on dedicated devices. However, eye gaze for tablets is improving rapidly. This advantage for dedicated devices is changing may change by the time you read this book.

One con of a dedicated device is they are very difficult to repair. The device must be returned to the company or manufacturer, meaning the user is without a voice for an extended period of time while the device is being repaired.

Dedicated devices are also very expensive to replace. They cost between $4,000 to $20,000, and it is cost-prohibitive for most families to purchase a new device until the insurance company agrees to fund it. Insurance companies and state funding will usually replace an AAC device every five years. During those five years, you are stuck with the purchased device and software whether it's a good fit for the user or not.

Limited software choices are another a con of a dedicated device. The user can choose between just a couple software packages when they purchase the device. You cannot easily change software or get a different device if the first one does not work out.

Dedicated devices are often heavy. Their weight is decreasing somewhat, but they are still heavier and bulkier than an iPad or tablet, especially compared to mobile options like an iPad Mini or iPhone Plus.

## Tablets

Tablets with an AAC app are also considered high-tech AAC devices. Tablets currently available are iPads, Android tablets, and Windows tablets.

A huge pro for tablets is the cost. Tablets are inexpensive and can be acquired for anywhere between $29 to about $800. Even the most expensive tablets are very inexpensive compared to the dedicated devices!

Tablets are also very lightweight. Many families have concerns about a heavy device, especially for someone who is able to walk and will carry the device. Tablets remain lightweight even with a heavy-duty case. I work with two kids who use iPhone Pluses for AAC. They are both very small children, but they are able to wear their devices in a crossbody bag called a CHAT Bag. With the CHAT Bag, it is easy for them to carry their AAC devices with them all the time. The system is lightweight and they have it with them 24/7 as they should.

Tablets can also be repaired or replaced in almost any city across the world. You can go into an Apple Store, Best Buy, or any computer store and have the problem diagnosed and repaired. If it cannot be repaired, it can be replaced quickly and much less expensively than a dedicated device.

The AAC app used with the tablet can also be easily replaced if it does not work for the user. For a maximum of $200 to $300, you can load a different app on the same device – much easier than buying a completely new dedicated device.

Another pro for tablets is the cool factor. Everyone is walking around with an iPad or tablet, so users do not feel different from their peers when they have a tablet for an AAC device. For kids, their peers usually think their tablet is really cool! We therapists and parents often have to set expectations of the other children not taking or touching the tablet. I have found if the user wears the tablet in a cross body bag, other children are less likely to touch or take the tablet.

A con of a tablet and AAC app is lack of funding or reimbursement by insurance. Tablets must be paid for out-of-pocket by families or through grant programs. None of the insurance companies or Medicaid managed care organizations I work with will reimburse or pay for an iPad, tablet, or AAC app. Hopefully, this situation will change in the future as physicians, insurance companies, and families realize the power of mobile technology for nonverbal patients.

Another con of using tablets for AAC is customer support depends dramatically on which app you choose. Some apps have significant support on their website and Facebook pages for families and therapists. Others – usually the less expensive options – do not have much support. It is important to investigate the level of customer support before you choose an app.

Mounting a tablet to a wheelchair can also be challenging. Based on the model of the tablet, the availability of mounts varies. Mounts can be purchased from Amazon or other sources, but they are not guaranteed to actually work – or work well.

As of the writing of this book (2017), eye gaze technology is not available for iPad or iPhone. Some eye gaze devices for Android exist, but they are not yet on the market for consumers. Eye gaze bars are available for Windows tablets and can currently be purchased by consumers. These eye gaze bars are made for gaming, not AAC, but hopefully that will change soon. However, these eye gaze bars are much less expensive because they are made for the gaming market and general population.

We have covered many pros and cons of the two types of AAC devices. The chart below summarizes these points:

| | PROS | CONS |
|---|---|---|
| **TABLET** | • Lightweight<br>• Inexpensive<br>• Easily repaired<br>• App / software easily changed<br>• "Cool" Factor | • Not funded by insurance<br>• May have less support |
| **DEDICATED DEVICE** | • Funded by insurance<br>• Support available | • Heavy<br>• Expensive<br>• Difficult to repair / replace |

# CHAPTER 2
# ACCESS METHODS

Once you have selected an AAC device, your next choice is how the user will access that device. Ease of access is a key indicator for success with augmentative communication, so this decision is also important. We will explore three access methods in this chapter:

| | |
|---|---|
| Touchscreen | User interacts with the device by touching areas on the on the display screen. |
| Switches | User interacts with the device using physical objects to make selections on the screen. Examples include buttons, levers, and sensors that can be activated with various parts of the body. |
| Eye Gaze | User controls a mouse or pointer on the device with his or her eye movements. |

## Touchscreens

The most common method of interacting with an AAC device is through a touch screen. Touch screens are amazing! It is easy for most people to activate a device with the tap or swipe of a finger. The user must have adequate use of his or hers hands and arms in order to activate the screen. If the user can use their hands, a touchscreen is usually the best way for them to access AAC.

At first, the user may have difficulty interacting with a touchscreen device. However, I've had much success in teaching children and adults to use a touchscreen even if they struggle with fine motor control. I have several patients who have come to me unable to accurately hit a target on a touchscreen. After therapy and practice with different apps on the touchscreen, my patients were able to choose from a field of at least four icons on a touchscreen.

One little boy that I worked with had cerebral palsy and could not accurately touch the screen. Because he also had a vision disorder, using eye gaze technology was extremely difficult for him. After a year of working with an iPad, he was able to choose between four icons reliably. Four choices can open up a large variety of vocabulary! The initial screen can have four folders which open into four *more* folders, which then open into more folders or vocabulary icons. It can go on and on. While not the most effective way of using a touchscreen, it can work! By using folders, we give users as much vocabulary as possible.

Another child I work with is a little girl with very poor fine motor skills. She learned to use a touchscreen and can now accurately target very small icons. Her fine motor skills are still very poor for everything *except* for her AAC system. She has success because she is very motivated to communicate! When we first started working together, she used an iPad Mini and could only select from a field of six choices. She now uses an even smaller iPhone Plus with the Proloquo2Go app and says complete sentences!

I recommend using a touchscreen if at all possible. It is the least expensive and easiest access method.

## Switches

Some AAC users may need to use switches as their access method. A switch is a secondary piece of equipment used to select icons or options on the AAC device. Switches are similar to using a mouse with a computer. Switches are available on dedicated devices and tablets running switch-accessible software.

Honestly, I think switches are the most frustrating and time-consuming way to communicate with an AAC device. It is ideally used only by people who have no other way to access AAC. An example is a user who is blind and also nonverbal. The user cannot see the screen, so he or she can use a type of technology called auditory scanning. This method speaks aloud the items and icons on the screen. The user listens as the scanner speaks what is on the screen and hits a switch when the scanner says the item they want to select.

Switches are also a viable option for patients who cannot use eye gaze technology because of motor difficulties but can hit a switch.

There are many types of switches. The most common switches are big buttons. Another popular type of switch is a leaf switch, which is very easy to tilt and tap. Joystick switches are another option, and they look like common video game controls. There are even pillow switches that can be positioned near the user's head. For users without the use of hands or arms, sip switches provide an interface with the device by blowing into or sipping on the switch like a straw.

To have success with switches, it is imperative to find someone who can help you decide which switch will work best for your child or loved one. The AAC user will also need to practice using the switch. Occupational therapists are very helpful in evaluating which switch will be the most accessible for the individual AAC user and helping the user learn to operate the switch.

## Eye Gaze

Some AAC users are more successful using their eyes to activate a screen. This access method is commonly referred to as "eye gaze." Eye gaze technology has improved dramatically in the past few years.

My friend and employee, Megan uses an eye gaze device for communication. She also controls her computer with eye gaze to complete schoolwork and tasks for my business. She even uses eye gaze to create art! Megan is a high school graduate and currently attends the University of Houston. She was in all general education classes throughout her public-school years.

Eye gaze can be used to perform any task on a computer or tablet. It is primarily available with dedicated devices, but some eye gaze devices are currently available for Windows tablets and computers. Android tablets will hopefully support eye gaze technology in the near future.

Eye gaze has a steep learning curve, but the learning is worth it for users unable to access an AAC device in any other manner. It is hard work for users to build the eye muscles to control the eye gaze device. They must practice daily and in frequent, short sessions to build these muscles. The user also must learn where to focus to select different areas of the screen. Much dedication and full-team involvement is necessary! It is also helpful to have a physical therapist assist with positioning for eye gaze access.

# Chapter 3
# INTERFACES

AAC devices use an interface to allow users to interact with the system. AAC interfaces can be classified into three types:

| | |
|---|---|
| Scene-Based | The app displays a photo or drawing of a room or scene. The person communicates by touching the photo on various "hot spots" that have been recorded with messages. |
| Text-Based | As the user types in words or sentences, the app reads the communication aloud. |
| Symbol-Based | The app uses photos or drawings to represent words or phrases. When the user presses the button, the word or phrase is spoken. |

These interfaces are available for dedicated devices and tablets. They also support all access methods – touchscreen, switches, and eye gaze. Let's learn more about each of these interfaces to determine which might be appropriate for your loved one.

## Scene Based Interfaces

Scene-based interfaces allow you to load a drawing or photo of a place onto the AAC device's screen. Hot spots – "clickable" areas – can be added to the photo or picture and a recording added for each hot spot. The recording can be a sentence, paragraph, or single word. When the user wants to speak, he or she activates that part of the photo.

I like to use scene-based interfaces for situations such as classroom presentations. If everyone in the class is getting in front of the class and talking about their vacation or what they did over the summer, it is wonderful for a child using AAC to also stand in front of the class, show a photo on their AAC device, and then press hot spots to "tell" what they did on vacation. For instance, they might have a photo of Disney World. As they press Cinderella's castle, the hot spot could say, "This summer, we went to Disney World. I loved Cinderella's castle." The child could then press another area and the device could say, "We went to Magic Kingdom, but we also went to Animal Kingdom." The child might also press somewhere else for the device to say, "I saw giraffes in Animal Kingdom."

You can also use household photos with scene-based AAC. Some ideas are to use photos of the refrigerator, a bedroom, or living room. The user can then request specific items shown on each of the photos.

Scene-based interfaces are great for younger children, as scenes often make more sense to them. This type of interface helps the child see and request objects in context.

## Text Based Interfaces

Another type of interface is classified as a text-based interface. These interfaces require literacy skills, and the user must be able to spell, type, and read.

Text-based interfaces rely on text-to-speech technology. The user selects words or types, and the app then reads the word or phrase aloud. Text-based interfaces are fully customizable with a variety of voices. Some interfaces even allow you to have two different languages. Text-based interfaces usually include both word prediction and sentence prediction, speeding up the communication process.

Text-based interfaces can be much faster for teenagers and adults with the ability to read and write. They are also extremely flexible because the device does not have to be pre-programmed with all the vocabulary the user might possibly want to say. The user simply types in whatever they want to communicate.

## Symbol Based Interfaces

The most frequently interface for AAC systems are symbol-based interfaces. Symbol-based interfaces can be arranged by either core words (words frequently used in the selected language) or categories.

For example, a category-based system would have categories for food, clothing, and actions. Some core words would also be available in folders so the user could build sentences.

Core words allow the user to have more novel communication, but category-based interfaces are often easier to access and find on the device. I usually combine core words and category-based vocabulary into one interface.

# CHAPTER 4
# CHOOSING A DEVICE

Choosing an AAC device means asking yourself many questions. The outline in this chapter is a summary of factors to consider when choosing a device.

Remember: AAC users are most successful when they have their device with them at all times. Plan now for how the user will carry their device. The choices you make when selecting a device will impact how easily your loved one accesses and adopts AAC.

**Cost:**

- What is the cost of the device?

- How will the device be funded?

- Can you afford to purchase the device out-of-pocket?

- Do you need to find a grant program?

- Do you need to use insurance or Medicaid?

- How important is the cost to you?

## Durability / Weight / Method of Carrying the Device:

- How durable is the device?

- How heavy is the device?

- Will the device be mounted to a wheelchair, placed on a mount that is moved around the home, or carried by the user?

  *(If mounted to a wheelchair, weight is less important.)*

- Will the user throw or drop the device?

- What cases are available for the device?

  *(Some Android tablets that are very inexpensive do not have many durable cases available.)*

## Repairs:

- If the device breaks, how and where can it be repaired?

- What will you do if the device breaks, is stolen, or becomes outdated?

- Are repairs covered by insurance or a warranty?

*(Consider the worse-case scenario; this factor is often forgotten when making a purchase decision.)*

## Interface:

What type of interface do you want?

- Scene-based?

- Text-based?

- Symbol-based?

## Access Method:

How will the user access the device?

- Touchscreen?

- Eye Gaze?

- Switches?

## Batteries:

- How long will the battery last?

- How and when will the battery be charged?

If choosing a tablet for an AAC device, you will need to choose an AAC app. Importation considerations for AAC apps are listed below:

**Apps:**

- Does the app require internet access?

- Is the app easy to customize?

- Are other family members, therapists, educators, nurses, and others willing to use the app?

- Does the app have customer service?

- Is the app you prefer available for / compatible with the tablet you like best?

# CHAPTER 5
# IMPLEMENTING AAC

Remember the beginning of this book when I compared AAC to a marathon? This chapter – and implementing AAC with your loved one – is where your marathon begins!

Let's continue the running analogy. Couch to 5K (C25K) is a running plan to transform a person from couch potato to runner in two months. The program even has an app that guides you through daily steps toward your goal. The idea is it takes baby steps, habits, persistence, and patience to run a 5K. The app helps the runner build stamina and strength while ensuring success through small steps. Implementing AAC can be done quite similarly.

AAC isn't an "easy" 5K; it is a difficult marathon. But just as completing a 5K is a step toward running a marathon, developing habits, taking baby steps, and having persistence and patience, can equip your AAC user to run the race toward communication.

## Expressive Language Development

Before we jump into how your child or loved one will process with AAC, let's review the typical sequence of expressive language development.

According to David Wood, Associate Professor from Carleton University, Canada, language acquisition takes place in six consecutive stages:

- **Pre-Linguistic** - During the first year of life, the child is in a pre-speech stage. The child learns to use gestures, eye contact, and produce non-speech sounds.

- **Holophrase** - This stage is also known as the "one-word sentence" stage. Typically developing children reach this stage between 10 and 13 months. The child begins to use some single words, but the meanings of the single words are dependent on the context of the situation and nonverbal cues.

- **Two-Word Sentences** - This stage is reached by typically developing child at about 18 months of age. In this stage, the child starts to combine words into two-word phrases. Examples of these simple sentences would be "more milk" or "big kitty." At this stage, children still use significant nonverbal communication to augment their speech.

- **Multiple-Word Sentences** - Typically developing children reach this stage between two and two-and-a-half years old. They begin combine multiple words into sentences and start to use some grammatical structure. Examples of these sentences are "I want more milk," or "Mommy go to work."

- **More Complex Grammatical Structures** - This stage is reached by typically developing children between the ages of two-and-a-half and three years of age. In this stage, children use longer phrases or sentences and use more sophisticated structure. They also use more functions of communication such as questions and prepositions. Examples of this stage are "Where is Daddy?" and "I can't play."

- **Adult-Like Language Structures** - Typically developing children reach this phase at about five to six years of age. At this stage, the child's expressive communication sounds very adult-like.

These stages of expressive language development can also apply to AAC users. While some users will jump quickly through these levels, many will follow the typical expressive language sequence. AAC is also much more difficult than verbal speech, and AAC users will often rely more on single-word utterances than phrases. It takes five to six years of practice for a typically developing child to reach conversational speech. It may take an AAC user many more years to reach a conversational level of communication.

Are you ready to begin your AAC marathon? Get started with these four steps:

## Step 1 – Get Off the Couch

The first step in implementing AAC is turning on the device. It may sound simple, but this step is a major one for many families. Technology can be intimidating, so you need to take a deep breath and turn on the device. Open the app or the software and look at it. Just these tasks may be enough for day one. It seems like so little, but it's a step toward communication!

The next day, turn on the device, open the app or software, and look at it again. Push some buttons. Don't worry – you're not going to ruin the device! Share the device with your child or loved one who will be the AAC user. Allow them to push some buttons.

If your child or loved one is proficient with the chosen access method (touchscreen, switches, eye gaze) and can interact with the device, you can move to Step 2. If not, you'll want to work on some basic AAC skills. Use fun apps or software games to train the person in cause and effect. If the AAC user is not reliable in activating a touchscreen or eye gaze device, use games to encourage and teach these skills. *Look 2 Learn* is a helpful software application available for eye gaze devices. It is great for working on cause and effect and device activation for eye gaze users.

For more apps and games that encourage and teach AAC skills, see Chapter 9: Apps That Encourage AAC.

## Step 2 – Customize the App or Software

You want your child or loved one to be successful with AAC. I have found customizing what the person sees when they first open the app or software is vital to success. I recommend starting small.

Although I want everyone to eventually have full core word vocabulary, seeing lots of words and icons on the screen is overwhelming to the AAC user and his or her family at first. By editing the app or device to just a few icons in the beginning, the AAC user can learn to communicate and experience immediate success. If the interface is overwhelming, the AAC user and family often feel defeated and will give up on the process.

Read more about how to start small in Chapter 6: First Boards

## Step 3 – Use the Device!

I often start with a screen (sometimes called a "board") of two to four choices on a new user's ACC app or software. These choices must be highly relevant and highly reinforcing for the user. It's important to start with choices that can be consistently reinforced.

I start by using this little board with limited choices in a structured activity for 5 to 10 minutes, twice a day, every day. An example would be a board for snacks. The snack board would be presented to the patient every day, each time the person is offered a snack. The choices should be snacks that person likes and is allowed. The snack board could have icons with goldfish crackers, pretzels, milk, and water. For each bite, the parent, caregiver, or therapist asks what the person wants. The child or adult then activates the touchscreen and makes a selection. Whatever snack or drink the person chooses, the caregiver gives.

What should you do if the person doesn't respond? I recommend offering verbal, visual, and then tactile cues. A verbal cue would be, "Tell me what you want." If no response, ask "Do you want goldfish or pretzels?" If still no response, point to the goldfish icon and then the pretzel icon. Finally, if the person does not respond, move his or her hand toward the touchscreen. Be patient, wait, and repeat.

The same method can be applied for eye gaze users, except giving tactile cues is very difficult with eye gaze!

## Step 4 – Take the Device Everywhere

It is very important to develop the habit of always having the device with the AAC user. It sounds very simple, but it is probably one of the most difficult steps in using AAC. The user must always have access to his or her device. My patients with the highest rate of success are the ones who have access to their devices at all times.

Even if the AAC user is not using his or her device consistently yet, start bringing it everywhere. Do not leave it at home. You are building the habit of keeping the device with the user, and it must be a priority for everyone involved in the child or adult's life. Just as you wouldn't leave the house without your phone or diapers, do not leave the house without the AAC device. I know it's hard – that is why I emphasize it as an early step in the AAC process.

The device must also be accessible. It should not be in a backpack, across the room, or in the car. The device must be with its user! A good solution for iPads, tablets, and portable dedicated devices is to use a harness or a strap. See www.chatbag.net for information about ChatBags . Larger dedicated devices or devices with eye gaze should be mounted on a wheelchair. You should also have a plan for using a floor mount or a table stand.

## Modeling

Modeling is also called aided language stimulation in the AAC world. It is simply using the AAC app or device to talk with the AAC user. In therapy, I normally model on the user's device, but you can also use a second device with the screen duplicated to match the user's. One of my therapists uses her iPad to model with her patients. She has her patients' devices duplicated on her iPad, and she even has a case with a strap that she wears during the session.

Modeling the use of an AAC device is so important to user's success. I model all the time during assessments and in follow-up therapy. I have been seeing Richard for AAC speech therapy for years. He composes complete sentences on his iPad and uses a large amount of vocabulary. I still model with him. In a recent therapy session, we learned some new core words, and now he can talk about things he did in the past or wants to do in the future. Because he is learning new vocabulary, I constantly modeled the correct use of this vocabulary throughout the session.

It is important to remember modeling isn't something you will do for just a few weeks; it will be helpful for years. I teach most AAC skills through modeling. When I do an assessment of a child or adult's potential to use technology for communication, I show them how to request and label using the AAC device or app. I do this by literally touching the device, activating the icon, and then verbally saying, "book". I then say, "I said 'book' with my iPad!" I use modeling very frequently when the user is new to AAC. I fade it out as the user gets better at using the device or app. As we add new vocabulary or new grammar, I model heavily again. I also strongly recommend parents model frequently.

## Possible Pitfalls

One of my speech language pathologist friends asked me, "What do you do if you model and the patient doesn't use the app or device?" The answer is to keep going! I reevaluate the app or device and the board or pages I am using. I keep modeling and keep trying. If the user doesn't seem to be making progress, I then reevaluate how the app or device is set up. Is there too much vocabulary or too little vocabulary? Is the vocabulary relevant to the user? Is there vocabulary that is motivating to the user?

If the user won't use the app or device after two to three months of very consistent modeling, I change the setup of the app or device. I put more relevant vocabulary and either add or hide some vocabulary. If the person using the device doesn't feel like the device is getting them what they want, they will likely be unmotivated to use it. Sometimes it requires a treasure hunt to find what motivates the user! After I figure out motivation and edit the device or app, I present the new vocabulary to the user and continue modeling use of the device or app.

I very sparingly use hand-over-hand assistance to force the user to choose an icon on the device. I will use hand-over-hand at the very beginning of implementing AAC if I am unsure the user understands the purpose of the device. When using hand-over-hand, I only work on naming. I help the user say "book" with the device through hand-over-hand assistance, and I then present them with a book. How does this look? I gently hold the user's hand and place it on the book icon to activate the icon. Then I verbally say, "Book. You used your iPad (or device, talker, etc.) to say 'book.' Here is the book." I hand the book to the AAC user. If I must use hand-over-hand assistance, I move as quickly as possible from this method to modeling.

# CHAPTER 6
# FIRST BOARDS

AAC can be extremely overwhelming in the beginning. If you do an image search for "AAC" in your favorite search engine, you will likely see screenshots of very complicated systems like these:

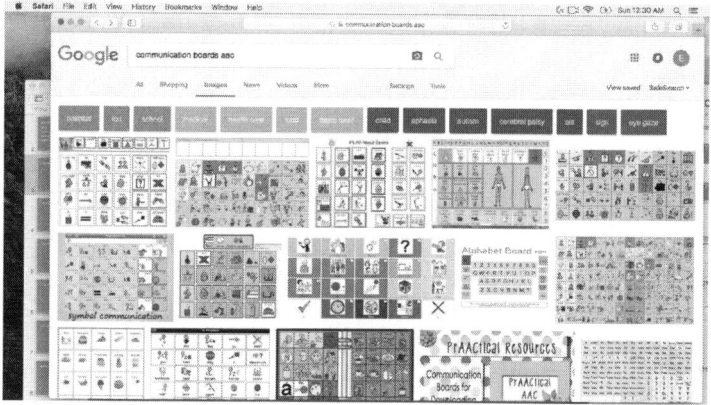

When your child or loved one's AAC device is powered on for the first time, it will look like some of these examples. There are so many icons on the page! There are so many colors! It's just too much from a sensory standpoint when an AAC user is getting started.

Complex AAC is great when you and your child or loved one understand the system. But for most people, it is way too much at the beginning. Even children and adults with excellent cognitive skills and age-appropriate receptive language skills have difficulty with these complicated pages. The person using AAC needs to first learn they have the ability to communicate, and then you can add more and more vocabulary, working your way to these more complex boards and systems.

## Boards

With your very first boards, you want to start small. You want to make the AAC device seamless for the user. Success begins with small, simple boards. I recommend you start with something like an "I want" page.

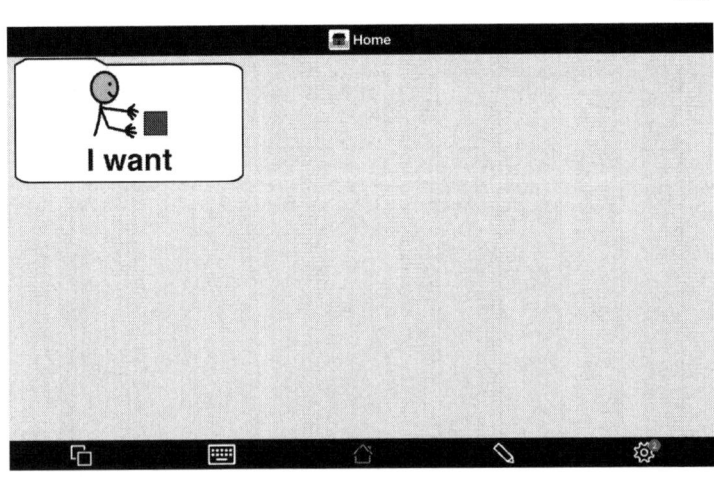

The image above shows the home screen on an iPad running the Proloquo2Go app. The organization of this app is similar to many other apps and devices. The home screen is where the user returns each time the app launches. This screen is an important one to consider in the beginning, as it is the user's first introduction to AAC.

I do not use "I want" in therapy as a carrier phrase, but I like using it for AAC because it acts as a placeholder on the home screen. With an "I want" folder on the home screen, the user taps the "I want" icon, and the app will open into another page like this one:

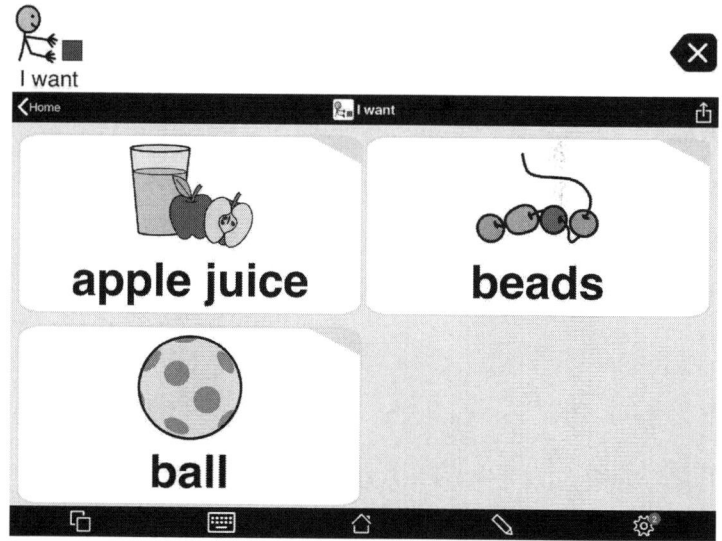

On this page you can put objects or activities that are very rewarding for your child or loved one. They will choose from these objects or activities in their first communications with you. You want to populate the screen with things that are very motivating for them to request, such as favorite toys or movies. It is also important to make sure you always have these items available so the user can be successful and can get the immediate gratification that their communication has been heard and understood. It is key at this stage that the child or adult knows you have heard their communication and that you are responding to it.

This page should have just a few choices – between one and four – in the beginning. Some users may start this small for just the first therapy session or hour at home. If they are successful, then you can add vocabulary as they understand how the system works and the power of their communication.

With the "I want" button on the home screen, it is also important to teach the user that he or she does not have to press this button for each phrase they want to communicate. I often model this situation for my therapy patients. I will say, "We are on the home screen. I am going to say 'I want.'" I then press the "I want" icon that opens the folder or page with their choices. If two of the choices are apple juice and cookie, I ask, "Do you want apple juice or a cookie?" and then model how to press the desired object. I also model the sentence for them by pressing the message bar and saying the sentence. As you can see, AAC requires a lot of modeling, and you will want to model the use of the device as much as possible.

Once your child or loved one is successful with a few vocabulary items, you want to add to their vocabulary. One of the problems with using just a few vocabulary items is that the user can only communicate what we have planned for them. You want to build the vocabulary available on the device as soon as the user can handle it. Adding more vocabulary means the user can progress toward communicating anything they want. However, adding vocabulary requires a balance. We do not want to rush them, but as soon as the user understands the system, more vocabulary should be quickly added.

Some of the next items to add are a board with up to six of their favorite activities. These activities should continue to be items you have readily available. Keep using the device at least twice daily at times when your child or loved one will need to make a choice among the items.

As you add some vocabulary, it's time to consider what kinds of folders and categories you want to use with the device. Some of the first boards might look like this:

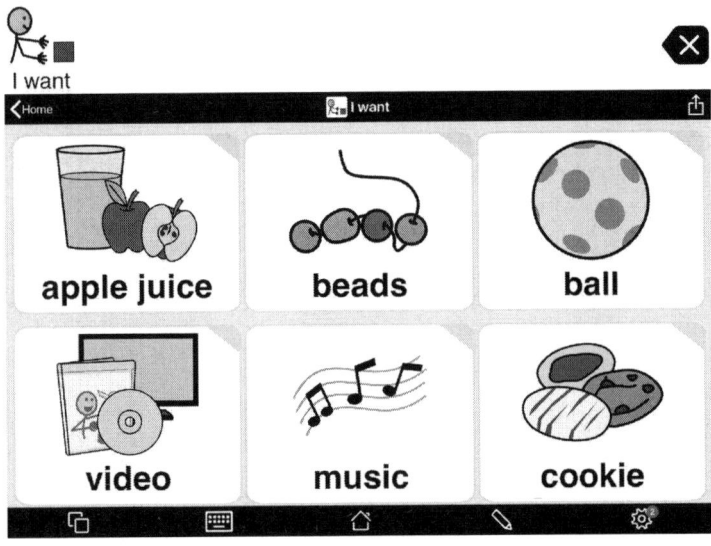

You may want to expand on your "I want" board by having a category just for snacks. In the beginning, the board may have just icons for cookies or chips. Every time the child has snack, you take out the AAC device and say, "What do you want? Do you want cookie or chips?"

Navigate to the home page and say "I want" as you press the "I want" button. The device says "I want" and opens to the snack page. The user can then choose either the cookie or chips icon.

The important thing is to model the communication every single time you have snack. Choose one activity, and then practice using the AAC device during that activity every time.

You might choose movies for that target activity. An example of a board for movies would include the choices for the user's favorite movies, like Finding Nemo or The Little Mermaid. To model this communication, you might say, "It's time for a movie. Which one do you want to watch? Let's go to the home page, and we'll say, 'I want.'" You press the "I want" button, and it open into the page with the movie choices. You then model, "I want Nemo," or "I want Little Mermaid."

A third example is using two favorite play activities like "music" and "ball." Every time the child has playtime, open this folder and ask them to choose between the two choices. Just as with the snack and movie example, use the AAC device each time you play together to reinforce the power of the communication.

Once the child or adult has success choosing desired objects and activities, it's time to add more vocabulary. We grow their vocabulary by adding more buttons and folders to the home screen.

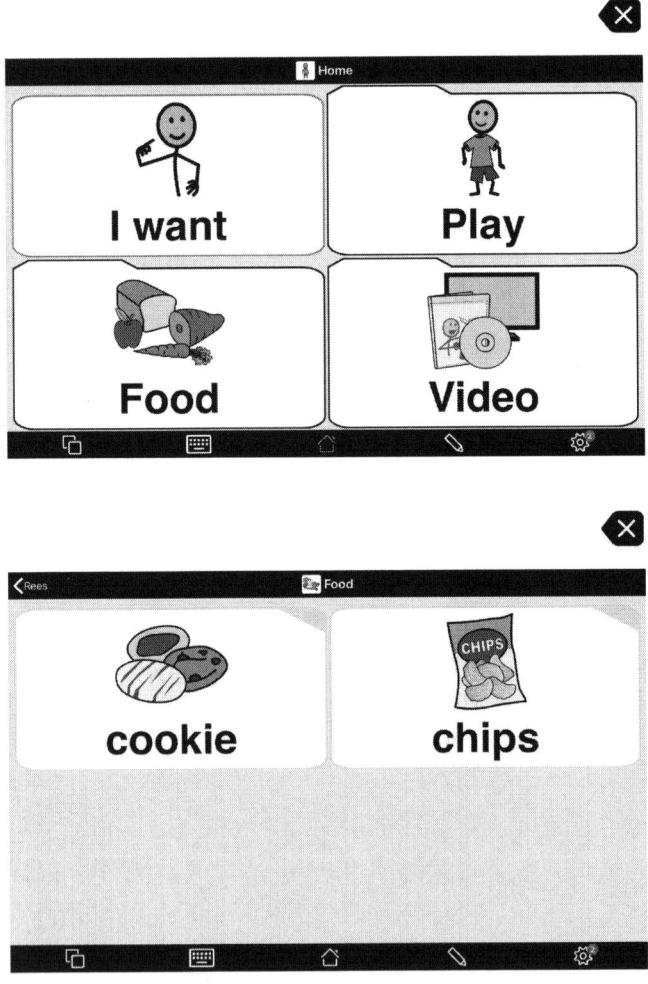

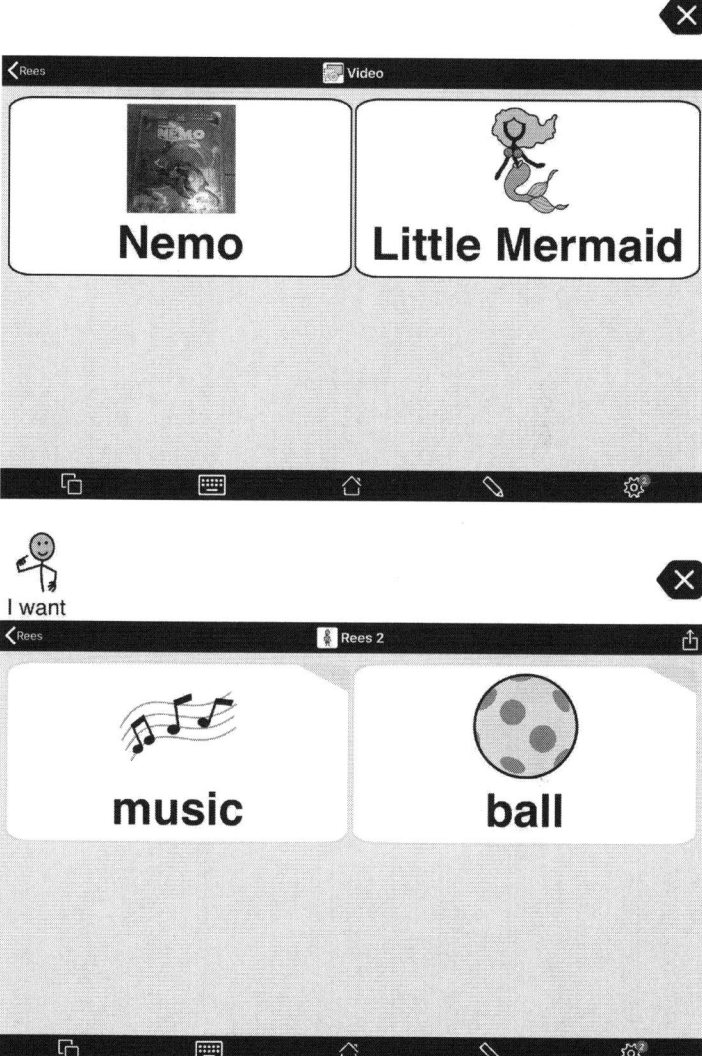

You can change "I want" into a button rather than a folder. Then add three folders to organize the vocabulary; for example, *Play*, *Food*, and *Video*. By organizing vocabulary into folders, we multiply the number of choices the user has and the ideas they can communicate. The communication is still very limited at this stage, because the user is can only communicate the things we have planned. However, as more vocabulary is added, an organizational system develops that will aid the user in finding what they want to say.

Here is another example. The home page has "I want" as a button and three folders of vocabulary. You could say, "Let's go to the home page. What do you want?" And if the user needed it modeled, you would press "I want" and then go to the folder they desire. You can tell the user, "I can say, 'I want ball.'" – and then model that sentence by pressing the "I want" button, the Play folder, and the "ball" button.

In the examples from this chapter, we progressed from one folder with two buttons to three folders with six choices, as well as the "I want" button. This method is how we build more and more vocabulary. Once your child or loved one is successful using the AAC device to communicate during one special activity a day, add a second and third activity.

## Organizing the System

Once you start adding buttons and folders, you are building a communication system, and you will need to consider how to organize the system. I have learned the hard way that if you do not plan ahead for when the user can communicate at the conversational level, you will have to re-work much of the organizational structure. When you're initially entering new vocabulary, be sure to ask yourself:

- How do I want these folders organized?

- What are things that a child this age – and two or three years older – want to talk about?

- What will the user want to talk about in a few years?

You want to ensure you build enough levels with buttons and folders so the user can access enough vocabulary to truly, functionally.

## A Caution About Yes/No

I discourage families from beginning AAC with "yes" and "no" buttons. Yes/No is a very complex concept, and it is often too overwhelming as a starting point for AAC.

Even people with good cognitive skills have some difficulty with Yes/No. Every Yes/No question isn't always a simple answer. Consider the question "Do you want apples?" Only having "yes" and "no" as possible responses does not allow for communicating the more complicated answer of "No, I don't want apples now, but I do want them later."

Yes/No can be helpful as the user progresses with communication, and it can be added to the AAC device at a later point.

# CHAPTER 7

# AAC APPS

Families implementing AAC have more choices than ever before when selecting a communication app for an iPad or tablet. This chapter discusses a few of the available apps and their features.

| | Platform | Interface(s) | Access Method(s) | Voices | Sharing | Languages | Other Notes |
|---|---|---|---|---|---|---|---|
| Proloquo2Go | iOS | • symbol-based core words <br> • topic-based <br> • keyboard with word prediction | • touchscreen <br> • switches | 60+ children and adult voices | • share messages with email, Facebook, Twitter <br> • copy/paste text into other apps | English Spanish French | |
| TalkTablet | iOS Android Windows Kindle Chromebook | • symbol-based <br> • keyboard | • touchscreen <br> • switches (iOS only) | large variety | • share messages with Messages (iOS), email, Facebook, Twitter | 15 languages | |
| CoughDrop AAC | web-based (all platforms) | • symbol-based core words <br> • keyboard | • touchscreen | large variety | • built-in messaging tools | 18+ languages | |
| Avaz | iOS (iPad only) | • symbol-based core words <br> • keyboard | • touchscreen | some variety | • share messages by text, email, Facebook, Twitter, but only platform can be used for sharing | 27 languages | • in-app instruction for parents <br> • data collection within app |
| Go Talk Now | iOS | • symbol-based <br> • includes videos <br> • no message bar | • touchscreen <br> • switches | large variety | | 20+ languages | |
| SonoFlex | iOS Android | • symbol-based core words <br> • topic-based boards <br> • keyboard | • touchscreen | 5 voices | | English | |
| TouchChat | iOS | • symbol-based <br> • keyboard <br> • visual scenes | • touchscreen | some variety | • share messages with email, Facebook, Twitter <br> • copy/paste text into other apps | English Spanish Hebrew | |
| Snap + Core First | iOS (iPad only) Windows | • symbol-based <br> • keyboard | • touchscreen <br> • switches <br> • eye gaze | some variety | | English Spanish | • includes a visual timer |

**Proloquo2Go** is one the oldest AAC apps. It is available for iOS devices (iPad and iPhone). I love using Proloquo2Go because it's easy to edit and modify the system for each user's needs. This app is very popular, and many therapists and educators are familiar with it. Proloquo2Go can work at an early communication level up to the conversational level. AssistiveWare, the parent company of Proloquo2Go, has over 50 hours of free online training available on their website (assistiveware.com) for users and therapists.

**Talk Tablet** is designed for many platforms and operating systems. It works with Android, Windows, iOS, and Kindle. Talk Tablet can be used successfully with people who have a wide range of disabilities. This app is a great option for AAC users that do not have access to an iPad or iPhone.

**CoughDrop** is a newer AAC app. The beauty of CoughDrop is that it is web-based, meaning it works with any device that has a web browser – Android, iOS, and Windows. Because the only commercially available eye gaze devices are Windows-based, CoughDrop is a great app to consider for someone who requires an eye gaze access method on a Windows tablet.

**Avaz** is another full-featured app available for iOS. Avaz has a unique parent training feature within the app that teaches parents, educators, and therapists how to navigate the system. This features is very helpful if the user does not have access to a speech pathologist with specialized AAC training.

**Go Talk Now** is available for the iPad. A unique feature of Go Talk Now is that it was developed for both touchscreen and switch access. The app also allows videos to be embedded in the buttons.

**SonoFlex** is an AAC app that is available for iOS and Android devices. This app has a lite version that is free. The lite version has limited functionality, but is helpful in evaluating the app and determining if it is a good option for your child or loved one.

**TouchChat** is available for iOS devices. This app is unique in that it has symbol-based scene-based communication boards.

**Snap+CoreFirst** is a very new app – released in 2017 – by TobiiDynavox. The app is symbol-based and includes keyboards and a visual timer.

**Speak for Yourself** is available for iOS devices. It has different interface than most other AAC apps. The interface is based on motor planning rather than dynamic category screens like Proloquo2Go. The icons in Speak for Yourself (and also for LAMP, another

AAC app) are based on the Unity language and are always in the same location on the screen. This functionality is great for users who rely on motor planning to find icons.

# CHAPTER 8
# SETTING GOALS

## Setting Goals

Setting goals is vital to success in any endeavor. The single most important indicator of a child's success is the parents' expectations. Expect the most of your child! Plan with structured and well thought out goals.

Erik Carter –

http://www.nasddds.org/uploads/documents/parent_expectations_D21.pdf

"We found that young adults with significant disabilities whose parents definitely expected them to obtain post-school work way back in high school were more than five times as likely to have paid, community employment within two years after exiting. When other factors were combined into our model, parent expectations still increased the odds of post-school employment more than three-fold. The unexpected finding was that these expectations were a stronger predictor than anything else we examined--student demographics; the social, communication, and independence skills youth possessed; even access to school programs and transition experiences"

"For example, Bonnie Doren and her colleagues (2013) found that parent expectations predicted not only work, but also graduation rates and postsecondary education enrollment for students with high-incidence disabilities."

Throughout my sons' lives, I have had goals for them. Starting in infancy, I was aware of what we needed to work on next. With my son Henry, that was sometimes a goal of living! Early goals were feeding goals. I made goals related to how much milk they would drink, how long they would nurse etc. I also made goals for sleeping! While not written, I also set goals for developmental milestones. I had a plan of where to go next. I had expectations and I made plans to get us there. Goals give you a plan to work on. They give you structure and they help you plan the steps toward the expected outcome.

Make goals for your child! Have high expectations and make the goals in small increments that lead your child toward their goal. Set your long term goals and then plan how to set short term goals to reach the long term goals.

I do not write SMART Goals for long term goals. My long term goals are more general and overarching and inclusive of the whole child. I use SMART Goals for my short term goals.

An example of a long term goal would be: Sam will use his ACC device to communicate at the phrase level with his family members, community members, peers and medical professionals to express his wants and needs.

We are expecting that he will be able to use his device to communicate with other people in many situations, with many types of people and for wants AND needs.

After you have set a long term goal (or several), start setting short term goals. You may want to set just one short term goal at a time. Think about your big long term goal and how you plan to get there.

Some short term goals may measure someone else's behavior besides the child. For example, you may want to set a goal that the device will be carried by, attached to a wheelchair or available to the child all the time. This is really out of the child's (or adult user's) control. It is vital that the user have access to the AAC device in order to use it!!!! And it must be consistently available or they cannot develop the habit of using the device.

## Smart Goals

SMART goals are very popular in the business world. This goal setting framework has helped me frame my business goals in realistic and achievable ways. This framework will help you focus on your goals for your child, give you a method of accountability, and help you meet the goals!

SMART is an acronym for:

S = Specific - Make your goal detailed and specific. This could include who, what, where, how, and when.

M = Measurable - Make your goal measurable. This includes details about measurements and tracking details.

A = Attainable - Make your goal attainable. You and your child should be able to be successful with the goal.

R = Relevant - Make your goal relevant. The goal should be meaningful to you and your child.

T = Time Bound - Make a time limit for your goal.

When you go through these five steps, you will really know your goal and understand how you are going to meet it. This thoughtful method of goal setting is very powerful!

## SMART Goals Practice

Write your goal:

Specific: Make your goal specific (who is involved, where will it happen, what will happen, when does this need to happen, how will it happen)

Measurable: How will you measure your goal?

Achievable: Can you reach this goal in a reasonable amount of time?

Relevant: Is the goal relevant to you and your child?

Time Bound: Does your goal have a time limit?

Example Goal:

Sam will use his AAC device to say "hi" to his teacher every morning when he enters the classroom for an entire week. This will be accomplished in a month.

Specific: Yes. Who - Sam and his teacher. Where - In the classroom. What - Say "hi" with his AAC device. When - Each morning.

Measurable: Yes. Every day for a week.

Achievable: Yes. He can activate the device and has said "hi" a few times.

Relevant: Yes. It will increase his AAC use and social language.

Time Bound: Yes: It will be accomplished in a month.

## Getting Going with AAC
## SMART Goals

communication circles
Your App Lady

SMART goals are very popular in the business world. This goal-setting framework has helped me frame my business goals in realistic and achievable ways. This framework will also help you focus on your goals for your child, give you a method of accountability, and help you meet the goals! SMART is an acronym for:

| | |
|---|---|
| **S** | **SPECIFIC** Include details such as who is involved, what will happen, when does it need to happen, where it will happen, and how it will happen. |
| **M** | **MEASURABLE** Include details about how you will measure and track progress. |
| **A** | **ATTAINABLE** Choose a goal where you and your child can be successful. Can you reach this goal in a reasonable amount of time? |
| **R** | **RELEVANT** Choose a goal that is meaningful to you and your child. Is the goal relevant to you and your child? |
| **T** | **TIME-BOUND** Make a time limit for your goal. |

When you go through these five steps, you will really know your goal and understand how you are going to meet it. This thoughtful method of goal setting is very powerful!

### SMART Goals for AAC

You can use the SMART framework to set goals for your child's AAC progress. Here's an example:

> *Sam will use his AAC device to say "hi" to his teacher every morning when he enters his classroom for an entire week. This will be accomplished in a month.*

Betsy Furler, MS, CCC-SLP
© 2017 All Rights Reserved

communicationcircles.com

# CHAPTER 9
# APPS THAT ENCOURAGE AAC USE

I love apps! I am actually obsessed with apps! I run my business with apps and my iPads and I love using apps in therapy. Find out more about all the apps I love on www.yourapplady.com and my Your App Lady Facebook page.

Apps are great for encouraging kids and adults to practice and use their AAC systems. While you can use almost any app to encourage AAC, these are some of the apps that I particularly like using in speech therapy for AAC use.

There are quite a few skills that are really important to work on when using AAC. These include motor skills and speech/language skills. There are so many apps that help with these skills but it is very hard to navigate the app market,

Here are a few of my very favorite apps that address these skills.

## Cause and Effect Apps

Cause and effect is a skill that you hear a lot about. It is one of the skills most people agree is essential for a child to learn for expressive communication.

Many children and adults who are nonverbal do not have the ability to cause an effect on the world. Because of this, they do not learn the skill of cause and effect. It is not necessarily a cognitive issue. It is frequently an issue of lack of exposure.

It is important to determine if the child or adult understands cause and effect and has it cemented as a mastered skill. Cause and effect is a base for many other skills they need to learn.

Cause and effect is simply doing something and making something else happen. If you push a button, the toy turns on. If you switch a light switch, the light turns on. It is a very important concept to understand.

Typically developing babies and small children learn this while they are playing with toys. Many of our kids cannot play with toys because of their motor impairments.

Therefore, they have never gotten a chance to learn cause and effect. Some kids with autism or other disorders just have not quite put it together and do not understand that they have an effect on the world. Sometimes, this is because their behaviors are different from the typically developing child. When they do something, they do not get the effect that they planned on. They have difficulty moving their bodies, so every time they do something, something different happens. Their movements are inconsistent, so the results are inconsistent.

There are a few apps that help teach cause and effect.

Baby Rattle Toy is a great app for cause and effect. It is by the developer, SelenaSoft, Inc. It is one of my very favorite apps. This app is simply a star that moves around the screen. When you tap the star, it moves faster. If you hit any place else on the screen, animals pop up. The child learns when they hit the screen, something happens and that they caused the action.

Photo Buttons by Sensory Smoothie is another great app. This was developed by a speech pathologist. It is great for cause and effect. It is a little more complex than Baby Rattle Toy. This app has buttons that pop up on the screen when you tap the screen. Then if you tap the button, it will turn over and say a word. This is a great app to also use for vocabulary development. You can customize all of the buttons, and as they turn over, the child will learn different words. I also use it for articulation therapy. For instance, if a child is working on "R" words, I can customize this app so all the buttons have "R" words on them. When they turn the buttons over, they hear an "R" word and can then repeat it.

Cause and Effect Sensory Light Box by Cognable is another great app. This one is great for kids who love different types of lights. As you touch the screen, the screen lights up in different patterns and in different colors.

It's a simple app, but it does have a lot of options of different types of lights, and kids and adults love it. They learn that when they touch the screen, the screen lights up. They are causing that action.

## Higher Level Cause and Effect Apps

Higher level cause and effect is when you make two or more movements, something happens. An example of higher level cause and effect is lining up dominoes. When playing with dominos, you have to line the dominoes up and then push the first and they all sequentially fall down.

I like to work on higher level cause and effect after the child understands simple cause and effect.

Here are some apps that I like to use:

The first one is called Toddler Sandbox by Sai Services LLC.

On Toddler Sandbox, you see a screen with sand on it. As you wipe off the sand with your finger, you find a vocabulary card underneath it. You have to wipe all the sand off the screen before you can move on to the next card.

With this app, kids are learning that they have to make several movements before they can see the card.

Another app I love for higher-level cause and effect is called Peeping Musicians. With Peeping Musicians, a song plays and one of these little monster musicians pops out from one of the sides of the screen. When you see a little piece of the musician, you have to touch him and then he comes out and plays his music. The child has to learn to look around and find the musician and tap it in the correct spot.

## Touch and Drag Apps

The next skill that I like to teach is called touch and drag.

For those of you who use a touchscreen yourself, you know this is important for many apps. It is a skill that is not quite as important for augmentative communication, it can help the child or adult use the AAC app in a more functional way.

Touch and drag is when you touch the screen and you pull the object over on the screen or pull an area over on the screen to do something else.

Children and adults with fine motor difficulties often have difficulty with touch and drag. They struggle to get their hand on the right spot, hold down, and move that spot.

Sometimes, kids and adults do not understand the concept of touch and drag because it is not something we do a lot in our real lives. It is something that has to be taught on a touchscreen.

My favorite app for touch and drag (and for many other skills) is Injini by NCSoft. Injini is an app suite. It has twelve different games that allow kids to work on a variety of skills, including touch and drag. The puzzle portion is my favorite game in the app suite for touch and drag.

Another app I love for touch and drag is The Wheels on the Bus by Duck Duck Moose. There are many Wheels on the Bus apps in the App Store and Google Play, but I love this one by Duck Duck Moose. It offers many options for touch and drag.

For instance, when you get to "the doors on the bus go open and shut," you touch the door and drag it open to actually open the door.

## Scrolling Apps

The next skill is similar to touch and drag. It is scrolling.

Scrolling is simply dragging your hand across the screen to make the screen move, or scroll over. To scroll, you do not have to touch the screen in a specific place which is what differentiates it from touch and drag. You just have to touch the screen and move it over. This is another skill that is not seen in the real world very often. It needs to be taught on a touchscreen device.

Children with fine motor skills have difficulty learning this just because they have to coordinate their cognitive thoughts with the movement of their hand. That can be very difficult for them.

It is a very important skill to learn when using an augmentative communication device touchscreen because you have to be able to scroll to get to all your vocabulary.

Cars in Sandbox: Construction by Thematica is a great app to use to practice scrolling. I love this app because it is a fun app with many scrolling options. You take a construction truck through a sandbox and do all sorts of fun activities with it.

My PlayHome by PlayHome Software is another one of my very favorite apps. I love this app for so many reasons. You can use it to practice scrolling because you have to scroll around the house. It is also great for vocabulary development.

There are several basic skills that a child can use to help them improve their augmentative communication use. I do not want your child to master these skills before you introduce augmentative communication to them. I want you to introduce augmentative communication to them and work on teaching these skills at the same time. In therapy, I often do this by making a page on their augmentative communication device or app that allows them to choose from one of these apps that teach these other skills.

Build a folder that says "I want to play" that opens on to a page with icons representing the target apps. They could choose to play one of these games for a reward and they would also be working on one of these important skills.

# CONCLUSION

I have been a speech pathologist for 25 years. The explosion of apps, iPad and other mobile technology in the past few years has revolutionized speech therapy. I am passionate about the power of technology in the lives of people with disabilities. I hope this book is helpful to you as a parent, a speech pathologist, a speech therapist or an educator. As you integrate technology into your routine, remember it is purely a tool; a magical, wonderful tool, but a tool none the less. Apps will never replace great therapists and great educators, but they can make life easier and more exciting!

Apps for communication can be life changing! By providing a communication solution to a child or adult who is nonverbal, you will change their lives. It takes patience and persistence and it is not easy but it is worth the effort.

# REFERENCE

Tips for using an iPad with AAC

This section is primarily based on features available on the iPad.

## Guided Access

Guided access is literally a lifesaver. Guided Access allows you to lock the child onto the app that you want them to work with or play with. With augmentative communication, that means you can make an iPad into a dedicated device. You can make it into a device that only does augmentative communication, if you like.

If you are using an iPad with your child for some other reason, for educational or organizational purposes, you can also lock them into those apps. It works on any app on the iPad.

The guided access feature keeps kids from hitting that home button (that round button at the bottom of the iPad that they all like to hit so much).

If your iPad is in guided access and you hit the round home button, the iPad will not do anything. The iPad is stuck on the app.

Another great feature of guided access is its timer. If you want to allow the child to play with an app for a reward, you can set a timer and they will only be able to play that app for a certain amount of time. Once the time is up, then the iPad will freeze and the child will not be able to use the iPad for anything else until it is unlocked with a password.

Android has similar feature called "Pinned Apps".

## Turning On Guided Access

Go to the settings on the iPad,

Scroll down and tap "General."

Tap "Accessibility", scroll to the bottom and tap "Guided Access"

Make sure Guided Access is on.

Open the app you want to lock the iPad or iPhone onto.

Triple-click the home button. (The home button is that round button at the bottom of the screen.)

Click "Start" and enter a passcode. Make sure you remember what this passcode is.

Make sure when you set Guided Access for your child that you are always hiding the iPad when you put in the passcode. Many of our kids are very good at remembering numbers. They will remember the passcode!

Guided Access is now enabled.

To remove Guided Access, press the home button again three times. Press the home button three times quickly to turn it off.

Enter the passcode and click "End".

## Speakers

Tablets have built-in speakers, but they are often not loud enough for augmentative communication, especially if the AAC user needs to communicate in loud places like the school cafeteria, restaurants or other public places.

External speakers can increase the volume of the tablet. Bluetooth speakers are easy to use, inexpensive and effective.

On the iPad, the Bluetooth settings are in the Settings app.

Pair up a speaker with your Bluetooth and then your iPad or your iPhone will use that speaker rather than the speaker on the device.

This is really helpful in loud environments. I like to use a little speaker that can be placed close to the child's mouth. The sound is coming more from their mouth than from the device.

I found three speakers that can be attached to a strap.

My favorite speaker is the Ion Clipster. It comes in many fun colors. At the time I wrote this book (2017), it was $15 on Amazon.

It is very easy to connect with your iPad or your iPhone. You can also connect these to an Android tablet or a Windows tablet.The speaker has a clip on it and it is very lightweight. It is easy for even a small child to carry around with them.

One of my friends uses a Ion Clipster. When they are in the car, they clip the speaker to the rearview mirror. When the child is in the backseat using her iPad to communicate with her parents, the parents can hear the child well because the speaker is up in front with them.

If the person you are talking to is far away, you can give them the speaker so they can have it close to them. This also works well if the AAC user was communicating with someone that was hard of hearing.

I also like the JBL Clip2. This one is a different shape. It also comes with a clip and can be easily clipped onto the AAC user's strap from the iPad or a backpack strap. I got the JBL Clip2 on Amazon.

The third speaker I like is the JS Portable. The reviews say that it is not quite as sturdy as the other two, but it is very cute. It looks like an acorn! If I was a teenage girl using an iPad for augmentative communication, I would want this cute acorn for my speaker. It is almost like a little piece of jewelry. The JS Portable has a wrist strap on it. You can attach that onto anything.

## Carrying Cases

The AAC device or tablet should be with the AAC user all of their waking hours. It is important to find the perfect way to carry it. It also needs to be protected.

I love Chat Bags. Most of the patients I see use Chat Bags to carry their tablets or iPads. The Chat Bag can hold the tablet with a heavy duty case and can be worn like a cross body bag. This bag is available from www.chatbag.net. The Chat Bags are customized for each customer. Each bag is made with custom fabrics, as well as a custom size to fit whatever type of tablet and case the AAC user has.

With a Chat Bag, the AAC user always has their device with them. It also protects the device from other people grabbing it or stealing their device. It is always attached to them, and it gives the person using the device ownership of the device and their voice.

Most kids and adults who have their tablets/iPads in CHAT bags do keep them on all the time. They feel very protective of their devices..

It is important to choose a well made, heavy duty case for the tablet or iPad. I order all my cases from Amazon. They are much less expensive than buying them anywhere else.

I usually choose a hard case with a softer material on the exterior of the case. That seems to be the best combination of materials to keep your iPad safe.

I also like the cases made of heavy-duty foam material with a handle. These cases are very lightweight and easy to carry, but very protective. You can get a Chat Bag made to fit onto a case like this. This case is also off of Amazon.

I also like LifeProof cases. Some of the LifeProof cases come with a strap. LifeProof cases are waterproof or water-resistant.

## Screen Protectors

You may want to consider a screen protector that reduces glare on the device. I use a screen protector that reduces glare on my personal iPads due to my vision disorder and the glare on the devices. If the AAC user has a visual impairment, I recommend trying a screen protector that reduced glare. I use the SuperGuardZ brand from Amazon.

## Suggested Goals for Speech Therapy

One of the most difficult things we do as speech pathologists is writing goals. Here are some of my favorite speech therapy goals for AAC based therapy.

### First Goals

Patient will choose one icon on an AAC app/device to request with 80% acc.

Patient will choose two icons on an AAC app/device to request with 80% acc.

Patient will use an AAC device to greet by selecting an icon from a field of six with 80% acc.

Patient will state his name using an AAC device by selecting an icon with his photo on it in a field of four with 75% acc.

Patient will activate iPad apps with an isolated finger to work toward the use of an AAC app with 70% acc.

Patient will use an iPad to name objects from a field of 12 with 70% acc.

## Beyond Single Words:

Patient will combine 2 -3 icons on an AAC app/device to make a phrase with 80% acc.

Patient will combine 3 - 5 icons on an AAC app/device to compose a sentence with 80% acc.

Patient will use AAC app/device to comment with 80% acc.

Patient will answer a simple what question about a story with 70% acc.

Patient will engage up to 3 conversational turns including conversation starters with caregivers and peers using an augmentative communication device in 4 out of 5 opportunities with 80% acc. Patient will use an AAC device/app to answer who/what/where questions with 80% acc.

Patient will use an AAC app or device to state her name, address and phone number with 3 different icons in a field of 32 in community and medical settings.

The AAC device will be customized according to the user's needs with 90% acc.

Patient will use AAC app/device to comment during a conversation with 80% acc.

Patient will use an AAC application on her iPad to ask for help with 80% acc.

## Case Studies

When working with people who are nonverbal, you must presume competence! Presuming competence means to always assume that a person is capable. While you have to guard against frustration, you also must assume that the person using AAC is capable of using it and continue persevering until they are successful.

Many people who are nonverbal have been communicating through their behavior for years. An AAC system and functional communication are new and different. They must be given the chance to learn the device and the time to get used to it. Many people also have to learn cause and effect and the power of communication. People who are unable to speak and have limited mobility may not understand cause and effect. They have never before had the capacity to cause an effect on the world and therefore, they have not learned the concept of cause and effect. Similarly, without verbal communication, they may have never learned how powerful communication is. Both skills can be learned through appropriate and intentional use of AAC.

## Mia - Her Mother's Words
## By Katy Schilhab

Its almost impossible to describe my beautiful daughter. Almost anything I write sounds "not enough". Mia was born early and very tiny. Throughout the first year of her life we realized that Mia had some delays that were unexplained. Nine years later they are still unexplained! After many years of searching she still has an undiagnosed disability. One of the many challenges Mia has had to face is the fact that she is nonverbal. A few years ago, through a series of beautifully timed events, we were led to Betsy Furler. Betsy introduced us to an application on the iPad that has given my daughter a voice. In the past few years Mia has been learning how to use the iPad to communicate. What a life changing tool she now has! Not only has this tool given Mia the ability to communicate her wants/needs/desires with us, it has also helped US learn more about her as well. We discovered the deep well of knowledge within her and that Mia is so much like so many other little girls. She often tells us she wants to go to Target, HEB, to see her grandparents, eat pizza for dinner, watch Frozen, have a "crazy bath night" in the big jacuzzi tub, that she hears a fire truck on our daily walks..... etc.! She has a lot to say and what a magical device we now have.... My daughter doesn't speak like most daughters do, but she speaks. And although the voice coming out of that iPad sounds computerized sometimes, its the most beautiful voice I have ever heard.

## D - Never Give Up!
## By Betsy Furler

D was referred to me for an Augmentative Communication Evaluation four years ago. At the time, he had no means of communication except for spitting. He has severe cerebral palsy and uses a wheelchair. He is nonverbal and cannot walk. D had a severe orthopedic injury that had gone unnoticed for many months. He was in terrible pain but no one knew because he had no way to communicate. As a result, he started spitting to communicate. When he came in for his evaluation, he was wearing a mask to keep him from spitting at me. He was very angry. During the evaluation, I was able to get D to successfully touch an iPad screen with his whole hand and I decided that it was worth a shot to start speech therapy with him with the goal of Augmentative communication.

We started therapy and his goals were focused on building his attention span and purposefully activating an iPad. We were able to get him an iPad with the app ProLoQuo2Go on it. D made slow but steady progress. He could only activate the screen with his entire hand so we presented only two choices at a time. He eventually stopped spitting but started grabbing objects and people. D learned cause and effect. He was also occasionally choosing icons on ProLoQuo2Go to choose apps to play. He was starting to be able to have some control over his life and his behavior started to improve. After over 200 speech therapy sessions, D is doing great! He isn't able to hold a conversation yet. But he is consistently choosing what activities he is interested in. He is using the iPad to say hello and goodbye. D is also learning to say "yes" and "no" which is a much more complex skill. He still grabs at times but he is no longer angry. He has control over some aspects of his life.

The last time I observed D with his therapist, I was amazed at his ability to use his iPad. He can scroll through multiple icons to choose an activity!!!! He is using one finger to activate the screen. When his dad came home from work, D grabbed the iPad very purposefully and used it to say "hi" to his dad! At that moment, I knew he got it! He knows the iPad is his voice and i anticipate that he will continue communicating more and more. I am so excited about his progress and can't wait to see what he will be communicating in the next few years!

D's story is so powerful because it started with a scenario that most people would have given up on. He had behaviors that made therapy difficult. He didn't understand cause and effect. He had trouble even accessing the touchscreen. He only communicated with spitting. I am so grateful that D's doctor referred him to me and I am so grateful that the therapists who work for me stuck with him. I am also thankful for D's parents and sister. They persevered. They believed in their child and kept encouraging him even when it seemed like he wasn't making progress.

The moral of this story is to never give up and to see the progress. Progress can be slow but it is there!!!!

Printed in Poland
by Amazon Fulfillment
Poland Sp. z o.o., Wrocław